"Simple, practical, powerful! This beau[...] cultivate greater mindfulness and com[...] with their children. Highly recommended!"

> —**Shauna Shapiro, PhD**, professor; and author
> of *Good Morning, I Love You, Violet!*

"If you're looking for insights and breakthroughs in your parenting and family relationships, Hunter Clarke-Fields's latest guided journal is a transformative journey to become the parent you always wanted to be, bringing out the best in your family and yourself."

> —**Christopher Willard, PsyD**, author of *Growing Up Mindful*,
> coauthor of *Alphabreaths*, and faculty at Harvard Medical School

"Our presence and awareness contribute to family happiness and resilience, and in turn influence how our children engage with their world. You could also say, for our children to one day live in a society with less conflict and more kindness, that lofty path begins at home. As dynamically presented in *Raising Good Humans*, rediscovering our sense of clarity and intention through a guided journal may in these ways allow us to raise more joyful, resolutely *good* children."

> —**Mark Bertin, MD**, developmental pediatrician, author
> of *Mindful Parenting for ADHD*, and coauthor of *Mindfulness
> and Self-Compassion for Teen ADHD*

"I can't imagine parenting without Hunter's wisdom, tender guidance, and essential tools! My number one parenting goal is to instill a nurturing, loving presence in my children so they can turn to it and seek refuge in it whenever they feel the need. Hunter's work guides me daily to reach this goal by cultivating that presence within myself, thus allowing me to offer it to my children."

—**Kara Hoppe, MFT**, author of *Baby Bomb*

"This is more than a journal, it's a journey where self-awareness becomes your superpower. Follow the bite-sized and practical insights within these pages and learn to face those parenting challenges with self-compassion and grace."

—**Lynyetta Willis**, psychologist, speaker, author, and founder of www.triggeredtotransformed.com

"A beautiful, spacious way to process and make sense of our own very unique, personal mindful parenting practice. With actionable prompts and open-ended questions, *Raising Good Humans Guided Journal* is sure to change the way you think about yourself, your children, and your ever-evolving parenting journey along the way."

—**Shonda Moralis, MSW, LCSW**, coach; psychotherapist; and author of *Breathe, Mama, Breathe* and *Don't Forget to Breathe*

NEW HARBINGER JOURNALS FOR CHANGE

Research shows that journaling has a universally positive effect on mental health. But in the midst of life's difficulties—such as stress, anxiety, depression, relationship problems, parenting challenges, or even obsessive or negative thoughts—where do you begin? New Harbinger *Journals for Change* combine evidence-based psychology with proven-effective guided journaling techniques to help you make lasting personal change—one page at a time. Written by renowned mental health and wellness experts, *Journals for Change* provide a creative and safe space to process difficult emotions, work through challenges, reflect on what matters, and set intentions for the future.

Since 1973, New Harbinger has published practical, user-friendly self-help books and workbooks to help readers make positive change. Our *Journals for Change* offer the same powerfully effective tools—without ever *feeling* like therapy. If you're committed to improving your mental health, these easy-to-use guided journals can help you take small, actionable steps toward lasting well-being.

For a complete list of journals in our *Journals for Change* series, visit newharbinger.com.

RAISING GOOD HUMANS
Guided Journal

Your Space to Write, Reflect and
Set Intentions for Mindful Parenting

Hunter Clarke-Fields, MSAE

New Harbinger Publications, Inc.

Publisher's Note

This publication is designed to provide accurate and authoritative information in regard to the subject matter covered. It is sold with the understanding that the publisher is not engaged in rendering psychological, financial, legal, or other professional services. If expert assistance or counseling is needed, the services of a competent professional should be sought.

NEW HARBINGER PUBLICATIONS is a registered trademark of New Harbinger Publications, Inc.

New Harbinger Publications is an employee-owned company.

Copyright © 2023 by Hunter Clarke-Fields
New Harbinger Publications, Inc.
5720 Shattuck Avenue
Oakland, CA 94609
www.newharbinger.com

All Rights Reserved

Cover design by Sara Christian

Interior design by Amy Shoup

Acquired by Elizabeth Hollis Hansen

Printed in the United States of America

25   24   23

10   9   8   7   6   5   4   3   2   1   First Printing

Contents

Part 4: Caring for Difficult Feelings

Part 5: Parenting Mindfully

Welcome

Welcome to this guided journal! Good for you for opening these pages and for the intention you hold to do this important work. I hope these pages become a place for you to understand yourself and your family more fully, and to process the inevitable hurts and wounds of being a human raising another precious human. I've seen many parents do this work through the Mindful Parenting course that I teach, and I've seen the benefits it brings to their families and to them. And I'm honored to be your guide on this journey.

You're here in this parent-child relationship—with pressure, overwhelming responsibility, baggage from the past, *and* the possibility of overwhelming love and a positive lifelong relationship with your children. As much as we want to jump to the joy, the pressures and challenges can bog us down. This journal will help you process these challenges and move toward more ease and joy. It will help you move toward that vision of the parent you want to be while still being authentically yourself. **Let's start with an honest assessment of where you are now *and* where you want to go.**

How do you feel about parenting now?

What are your frustrations?

_____

_____

_____

_____

_____

_____

_____

_____

_____

_____

_____

_____

_____

_____

_____

_____

_____

_____

What do you want to feel instead?

What would you like to change?

_____

_____

_____

_____

_____

_____

_____

_____

_____

_____

_____

_____

_____

Mindful Parenting Manifesto

- A Mindful Parent is a new generation of parent: present, evolving, calm, authentic, and free.

- Mindful Parents reject the culture of "not good enough," knowing that when we free ourselves from unnecessary stress and limiting stories, our authentic, peaceful nature shines through.

- Mindful Parents practice self-compassion and see their challenges as teachers, not flaws.

- Mindful Parents value wisdom over reactivity, empathy over obedience, and begin anew every day.

- Mindful Parents live what we want our kids to learn, knowing that the best parenting is in modeling.

- Mindful Parents go within and get quiet to access their power.

- Mindful Parents practice presence, create their experience, embrace imperfection, and love themselves.

- Mindful Parents are motivated, knowing that with every step they are changing things for the generations that follow.

- I am a Mindful Parent.

Take a few moments to respond to the Mindful Parenting Manifesto. Where do you see your own strengths in this manifesto? Where do you see your challenges (a.k.a. your opportunities for growth in living as a mindful parent)?

PART 1

Keeping Your Cool

Many parents look at the challenges, irritations, and frustrations of parenting and blame their children. If we could only "fix" our children, life would be better. But instead of blaming your child—or yourself—I invite you to look at the difficulties and stresses of parenting as your *teachers*: as things to learn from, rather than things you wish would just go away.

Rate your current stress level as a parent:

1 2 3 4 5 6 7 8 9 10

What might be impacting your score?

_____

_____

_____

_____

_____

_____

_____

_____

_____

_____

_____

_____

All Parents Lose It Sometimes

You can feel it. Your heart beats faster, your blood pressure goes up, and your breathing rate increases under stress. "Losing it" happens when we have fast, automatic reactions because our brains have mistakenly perceived a threat. There are biological and evolutionary reasons why we lose it. In fact, when you look at it from an evolutionary perspective, I would argue that *it's not even your fault* when you lose it. Conflicts with our kids can *feel* threatening and trigger these automatic biological reactions. But while we don't "choose" to have this response, we *can* choose to temper its effects.

Write about a time when you were stressed, what you felt in your body, and how you reacted to the stressful situation.

Losing It Isn't a Choice

Losing control isn't a conscious choice that you make. It's your biological system reacting automatically. That means it takes intentional *practice* to learn to respond differently. It also means that we are not entirely to blame for our own reactivity. Reacting instantly to threat may have been critical for our ancestors. Our brain doesn't know that we live in a different world today.

This is also why most parenting advice doesn't take hold. Parenting experts largely neglect to teach us how to take care of our stress response. So when the going gets tough and we're stressed, we can't access whatever parenting techniques we might've learned. It all seems to fly out the window when our stress response kicks in. We're left feeling frustrated. We might even decide we're "bad" parents. But hear me now: There is nothing wrong with you! It's just your biological response—and there are tools to cope with that.

What happens when you lose it with your kids? Can you identify your thoughts in the heat of the moment? What do you feel in your body?

_____

_____

_____

_____

_____

Getting Off Autopilot

We spend most of our time with our children in automatic pilot mode, our minds fixed on accomplishing goals, solving problems, or planning and strategizing for the future. You might be planning dinner, for instance, while your child is telling you about their day. But when you're in that automatic doing/achieving/planning mode, your mind is likely elsewhere and you're probably not really in the present moment with your child.

And when we're not fully present with our children, we miss the chance to attune to their cues about what is happening with them, like a signal that our child really needs a hug or help regulating their emotions.

What if we started to practice mindfulness instead? Bringing our attention to the present moment, with kindness and curiosity? Bypassing the whole host of problems that arise with distraction?

Can you think of a time you weren't fully present with your child? Write about it here, including how you reacted to them and how they reacted to you.

What might have been different about the situation if you had been present with your child in that moment? Would there be a different outcome?

Mindfulness:
The Superpower Parents Need

"Mindfulness is awareness that arises through paying attention, on purpose, in the present moment, non-judgmentally."
—Jon Kabat-Zinn

Write down some initial thoughts you have about mindfulness. What does that word mean to you?

_____

_____

_____

_____

_____

_____

_____

_____

_____

_____

_____

_____

_____

_____

_____

_____

Ultimately, mindfulness—nonjudgmental present-moment awareness—is a quality we are aiming for; mindfulness meditation is the tool for building that quality in ourselves, and calming down our reactivity. "Meditation" can mean many things to people; for our purposes, I'll define it as a practice of training the mind to become less reactive and more present.

How do you practice mindfulness meditation? You deliberately focus your attention on what is happening in the here and now, aiming to be *more* attentive to the present moment rather than distracted. You practice noticing what's going on moment to moment, within you and around you, with kindness and curiosity—nonjudgmentally. Let's try it now so you can experience exactly what I'm talking about.

Before you begin, take a moment to rate your current stress level.

PRACTICE: Sitting Mindfulness Meditation

● **Find a quiet time and place.** Sit up tall on a chair or a cushion. Sit upright but relaxed. Be comfortable! You can even meditate in a recliner. But set a timer for 1-3 minutes so you don't have to worry about the time. Then, either cup your hands, letting your thumbs touch, or simply rest them on your legs.

● **Close your eyes fully or leave them at half-mast.** Bring your attention to a neutral sensation in the present moment, like your breath or the feeling of your hands touching your legs. Let your mind be spacious and your heart be kind and soft. Feel your breath at your belly or your nose, letting it be natural. Notice each in-breath and notice each out-breath. Say to yourself "breathing in" as you breathe in and "breathing out" as you breathe out. For some of us, the breath is not conducive to calm attention. If that's the case for you, direct your attention to a different "anchor" in the present moment like the feeling of touch or the sounds you hear.

🌸 **Expect your mind to wander right away.** That's normal! The goal is not to stop your thoughts but to train your attention. It's to spend more time in the present moment and less time lost in distraction. Label your thoughts "thinking" if you want, then return your attention to your breath. Do this again, and again, and again, and again, without judging yourself (it's just part of the process!). Each time you discover your mind has wandered, it's an opportunity to do a "rep" and build that mindfulness muscle. And even if you think you are doing this badly, you're still making progress.

🌸 **Meditation thrives on practice and a kind approach.** If you do this simple practice every day, you will gradually become more grounded and aware.

Take a moment to reflect on how you feel after your first practice.

Now, rate your current stress level:

1 2 3 4 5 6 7 8 9 10

Is it different from your earlier stress level? What changed?

Mindfulness meditation has many benefits and effectively zero negative side effects. Researchers from Johns Hopkins University found 47 studies that show that mindfulness meditation can help ease psychological stresses from anxiety, depression, and chronic pain.[*] More research has shown that it increases positive emotion,[**] increases social connection and emotional intelligence, and, importantly, improves your ability to regulate your emotions[***] (this is just what parents need!). I've seen all these benefits in my own life and in the lives of my students. Put simply, practicing mindfulness gives us the sense of equanimity and the groundedness we need to parent well.

---

[*]   Corliss, J. 2014. "Mindfulness Meditation May Ease Anxiety, Mental Stress." Harvard Health Blog, January 8. https://www.health.harvard.edu/blog/mindfulness-meditation-may-ease-anxiety-mental-stress-201401086967.

[**]   Davidson, R. J., J. Kabat-Zinn, J. Schumacher, M. Rosenkranz, D. Muller, S. F. Santorelli, F. Urbanowski, A. Harrington, K. Bonus, and J. F. Sheridan. 2002. "Alterations in Brain and Immune Function Produced by Mindfulness Meditation." *Psychosomatic Medicine* 65(4): 564–570.

[***]   Fredrickson, B. L., M. A. Cohn, K. A. Coffey, J. Pek, and S. M. Finkel. 2008. "Open Hearts Build Lives: Positive Emotions, Induced Through Loving-Kindness Meditation, Build Consequential Personal Resources." *Journal of Personality and Social Psychology* 95(5): 1045–1062.

Taking Mental Shortcuts

We don't notice it, but we take a lot of mental shortcuts in family life by using labels. These can be helpful, but they can also bias us in ways that make parenting harder. For example, if we've labeled one child as the "athletic one," and another as the "smart one," we limit the possibilities for these children. While it's natural to categorize and compare, we can take our labels too literally. Our preconceived notions about our children get in the way of *really* seeing them. Labels are also static, whereas our kids are always changing. Finally, our preconceived ideas can become self-fulfilling prophecies, particularly when they're negative—our children live up to those expectations. Yikes!

What are some labels that you or family members attach to your children? Why?

Another, more positive way we take shortcuts is with routines. Family life is often repetitive: make dinner, clear the table, do the dishes, get ready for bed. These routines help us get through life with more ease. The downside is that we can lose our ability to see things with freshness. Often we walk around all day with our heads bent over a screen. We don't appreciate the beautiful sky or the blooming daylilies. What's worse, we miss the sense of curiosity that children naturally bring to the world around them.

Generally, we're at our worst in the parenting department when we're in reactive mode. Imagine if, instead of that automatic pilot reactivity (and, say, your mother's voice coming out of your mouth), you could respond thoughtfully in those reactive moments. How might that change things?

Think of an example of a time when you reacted to your child on autopilot. Write down how you responded.

Now, write down how you wish you had responded. What might make the difference between reacting on autopilot and reacting more mindfully?

PART 2

Untangling Your Story

We all experience situations in which a child's behavior triggers an outsized reaction in us. Many times, it's because they've touched an old story of ours or some unresolved issues that could use a little healing and attention. In the pages that follow, you'll explore harmful patterns that may have been passed down through the generations in your family. As you open your eyes to these generational patterns, let them motivate and teach you. It's not magic, and it can be uncomfortable, but the benefits of examining old patterns to heal and create new ones are enormous. I've seen it happen time and time again with my Mindful Parenting students—by exploring your past and working through what you find, you can change harmful patterns for generations to come.

Kids Bring Up Our Stuff

The early years of parenthood can make us feel like we've totally lost our marbles. We are under intense psychological strain. We're back in a parent-child relationship and it's hard to recognize when we're bringing all our baggage from the past. For me, when my daughter didn't listen, it brought up my unresolved issues around not feeling heard. But at the time, I had no idea this was going on. Anger would well up like I hadn't felt since I was...a child. Because I hadn't done the work to excavate and understand what was triggering me, I blamed my daughter. What's wrong with *her*? Why won't she listen to me? It was clearly all her problem. If I could fix *her* behavior, then everything would be better. Right?

Write down something your kid does that elicits an outsized reaction in you.

Like little spiritual masters, children have an uncanny ability to reveal our unresolved issues. Something about your parenting experience is driving you bananas? There's your inner work.

If you dig deeper, what do you think it is about their behavior that you find so intolerable?

_____

_____

_____

_____

_____

_____

_____

_____

_____

_____

_____

_____

_____

_____

When we understand *why* we are so reactive—what old patterns and wounds are being triggered for us—then we can practice healing and choose a different way of being, rather than repeating dysfunctional family patterns. Then we have a chance to refrain from unwittingly passing this baggage onto our kids.

Understanding why you are triggered will help you respond more thoughtfully. *Without awareness*, we react out of old conditioning—that's when your own parent's voice, or the voice of your worst self, flies out of your mouth.

Transforming What You Transmit

If we never look at our old wounds and triggers, we'll continue to respond out of habit from the past, and probably pass our hurts down to our children. In fact, there's a saying, "What we don't *transform*, we *transmit*." Becoming conscious of these wounds will allow us to carry our own baggage rather than passing it down the generational line. Think of this as an opportunity to heal wounds not only for yourself, but for generations to come.

What was your childhood like generally? What was your relationship with your parents like?

_____

_____

_____

_____

_____

_____

_____

How did your parents discipline you as a child? What were their expectations of you?

Do your childhood experiences impact how you parent? How so?

What does the impact of your childhood experiences teach you about how you want to parent?

_____

_____

_____

_____

_____

_____

_____

_____

_____

_____

_____

_____

You can take this work deeper with the questions in _Raising Good Humans_, the book _Parenting from the Inside Out_ by Dan Siegel and Mary Hartzell, or with a therapist. Don't be afraid to move toward understanding and healing!

PART 3

Practicing Compassion

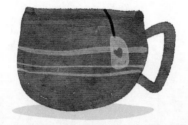

Do you ever find yourself trying so hard that you end up feeling grumpy and judgmental toward both yourself and your child? Without self-compassion, we tend toward harsh self-criticism, becoming both the attacker and the attacked. We are also less likely to try something new, because the mistakes we make—which are human and inevitable—lead to harsh self-criticism and discouragement. All this keeps us well and truly *stuck*, rather than doing what it really takes to parent well: getting up each time we fall and beginning anew. The ability to do that starts with compassion—being kind to ourselves, acknowledging our own struggles, and empathizing with the struggles of our kids.

Your Inner Voice Matters

What we say to ourselves in the privacy of our own thoughts really *matters*. Think about it this way: If I have an orange, what will come out when I squeeze it? Juice, of course. But what kind of juice will come out? Not pomegranate or kiwi. Orange juice. And like that orange, when we are squeezed, *what's inside is what will come out*.

What comes out of *you* when you are squeezed? That inner wicked witch? If your inner voice is harsh and critical, then that's what's likely to come out with your children too. For me, in moments when I was really squeezed, harshness and negative, disparaging criticism came out, because that's what was inside at the time. Often, it left me feeling completely incapacitated.

When your inner voice is harsh and mean, how do you feel? What kind of person are you then? What kind of parent?

_____

_____

_____

_____

_____

_____

_____

_____

_____

_____

_____

_____

_____

_____

_____

_____

_____

_____

Rate your current level of happiness or ease as a parent:

1 2 3 4 5 6 7 8 9 10

What might be impacting your score?

_____

_____

_____

_____

_____

_____

_____

_____

_____

Imagine if, instead of self-shaming, we could offer ourselves the kindness and understanding of a good friend. It may feel weird, but when we talk to ourselves kindly, we're able to downregulate our nervous system threat response that kicks in. We're also able to recover faster, pick ourselves up, and try again. And when we try something new and inevitably make a mistake, the soft landing that kindness gives us helps us to begin anew and try again. The truth is, it's far more practical to practice *self-compassion*—the practice of treating ourselves with kindness and understanding—than it is to be hard on ourselves.

When we practice self-compassion, we tap into our innate nurture system and naturally become more effective and responsive parents. As you develop more compassion for yourself, you'll have more compassion for your child and everyone around you.

What are kinder things that you *could* say to yourself when you mess up? (Hint: What would you say to a dear friend who felt badly?)

1. _____

_____

_____

2. _____

_____

_____

3. _____

_____

_____

4. _____

_____

_____

5. _____

_____

6. _____

_____

_____

7. _____

_____

_____

8. _____

_____

_____

When you mess up, do you tend to think that it's *just you* who does this? Part of self-compassion is reminding ourselves that *everyone* makes mistakes and has bad parenting days. I do; every psychologist, author, and expert does. Remember that you are not alone.

Stop Trying So Hard

Chances are you've been trained from childhood toward achievement and goalsetting. When we are so accustomed to striving like this, it becomes hard to simply rest in the present moment with whatever is going on. We tend to say to ourselves, "If only I were"—more calm, more intelligent, or a harder worker, in better health, wealthier, the list goes on—"*then* I would be okay. But right now, I'm not okay." The feeling of NOT being okay drives us to improve, right now! This sets us running on a hamster wheel of insecurity—and, as with all hamster wheels, we run and run and get nowhere.

Instead, I'm going to ask you to cultivate the attitude of *nonstriving*.

Letting go of striving (which is always directed at some future state) helps us become more present to what is actually happening. It's truly healing and restorative for us to let go of our agendas from time to time and simply let life unfold. Our children also thrive when, instead of constantly shuttling them from place to place, we give them space to just be.

Do you strive for perfection? What do you tell yourself about striving? How does it feel inside?

_____

_____

_____

_____

Nonstriving does not mean inaction, but instead holding things lightly. What are some areas in your life where you could ease up on the striving and hold things more lightly?

Practice Loving-Kindness

One life-changing way to build your compassion muscle is through the ancient practice of loving-kindness, either through formal meditation or compassionate thoughts you pepper throughout your day. The term "loving-kindness" is a translation of the Pali word "metta," which means "friendly, amicable, benevolent, affectionate, kind, or sympathetic love." It's the perfect antidote to that mean voice inside.

How do you practice? You start by simply generating the feeling of loving-kindness toward someone who's easy to love. Then you practice extending it to yourself, and to those with whom you have difficulties.

Loving-kindness is a form of love that is active. It's a way to look at ourselves and others with kindness instead of reflexive criticism.

- **Sit in an alert and comfortable position.** Let your mind be spacious and your heart be kind and soft. Let your body relax.

- **Feel your breath travel in and out of your body.** Notice any thoughts that pop up, then refocus your attention on your breath.

- **Notice any emotions that are present.** Let your body soften a bit as you exhale.

- **Picture someone in your life that has truly cared for you,** someone who is easy to love. Picture this person in your mind and recite the following phrases:

May you be safe.

May you be happy.

May you be healthy.

May you live with ease.

- **You are welcome to adjust the words.** Repeat the phrases over and over, letting the feelings come fully into your body and mind.

Now, practice loving-kindness toward yourself. You can picture yourself as you are now or picture yourself as a four-year-old child. Say to yourself the following phrases (or a variation that resonates with you). As you repeat these phrases, you can picture yourself suffused by the light of loving-kindness:

May I be safe.

May I be happy.

May I be healthy.

May I live with ease.

At times this practice may feel rote or awkward. It may even bring up irritation. If this happens, it's especially important to be patient and kind toward yourself. Accept what arises with a spirit of friendliness.

Once you feel you have established some sense of loving-kindness, expand your meditation to include others: friends, community members, all beings on earth.

You may even include the difficult people in your life, wishing that they, too, be filled with loving-kindness and peace.

Take a moment to reflect on how you feel:

_____

_____

_____

_____

_____

_____

_____

_____

_____

_____

Now, rate your current level of happiness or ease:

1 2 3 4 5 6 7 8 9 10

Is it different from your earlier level of ease? What changed?

_____

_____

_____

_____

_____

_____

_____

_____

_____

_____

As you make loving-kindness a part of your life, you'll gain more peace, ease, and kindness, and you'll naturally give that to others more frequently. As shame researcher Brené Brown wrote in her 2017 book *Daring Greatly*, "We can't give people what we don't have. Who we are matters immeasurably more than what we know or who we want to be."

PART 4

Caring for
Difficult Feelings

Difficult feelings are where the rubber meets the road in parenting. After all, it's pretty easy to be a great parent when everything's going well. What about when your child has a tantrum in front of your neighbors? Or when frustration takes over and you can't tag out? We need tools for caring not only for children's difficult feelings, but also our own—because our kids are watching what we *do* far more than what we say. This may be a learning curve for you, just as it was for me, because you may not have been taught much as a child other than "Don't cry," or "Go to your room." Remember, it's all a *practice*—and what you practice grows stronger.

Unhook from Negative Thoughts

Getting caught up in negative thoughts can prevent you from doing things that are important to you, like paying attention to your child.

Close your eyes and listen within. What thoughts do you have about yourself as a parent?

Thoughts like *I'm not good enough*, *I'm a terrible parent*, and more can "hook" our attention and distract us from being present with our children and making good choices. We can take our mindfulness into daily life by interrupting these unhelpful thoughts with acknowledgment. Here's how:

1. Do you notice yourself getting tight, constricted, irritated, or sad? Notice if there is a thought behind that, like *I'm terrible at this*, or *There must be something wrong with my child*.

2. Mentally put the phrase, "I'm having a thought that…" in front of the unhelpful thought, as a way to distance yourself from it so you can recognize it for what it is: just a thought.

3. Breathe, and choose your next action from a place of clarity.

Now, take a moment to sit quietly and use the steps above to "unhook" from your negative thoughts. How does it feel? What do you notice?

_____

_____

_____

_____

_____

_____

_____

_____

_____

_____

_____

_____

Unhooking from negative thoughts doesn't mean that they will go away forever. On the contrary, our minds will continue to tell us stories, and unhelpful thoughts will inevitably arise again. However, practicing the skill of unhooking from these thoughts, when they arise, can help us choose our actions with more intention.

Mindfully Taking Care of Difficult Feelings

When we're upset, we obviously don't want to feel that way, so blocking or fighting those feelings is our instinctive response. We want to avoid uncomfortable things. The problem is that we can't avoid all of life's hurts, and our resistance to them when they arise makes things worse.

Accepting the reality of painful feelings helps us heal. As counterintuitive as it may seem, when we accept and stay with that uncomfortable "I've got to get out of here" feeling, it often lessens, and sometimes completely disappears. Think about it as going to your edge, and softening.

Before you begin the next exercise, take a moment to rate your current stress level.

RAIN, a practice from meditation teacher Tara Brach, can help you remember the mindful way through difficult emotions. RAIN stands for "recognize," "allow" (or "accept"), "investigate," and "nurture." At first, you'll need a quiet space and some time to do this, but with practice, you can use RAIN to process feelings almost anywhere. Try this practice now. Thinking back to the last time you had difficult feelings arise...

- **Recognize.** Take a pause and mindfully breathe. Recognize that you are (or were) having a hard time. Recognize the sensations and feelings that are most prominent. You may notice a tight chest and shoulders. You might say to yourself "upset," "frustrated," or "hurt."

- **Allow (or accept).** Give yourself a moment to be with this emotion and feel the sensations in your body. If you're noticing a lot of resistance—that "no!" feeling—you can try saying "yes, yes, yes" to yourself instead. It's okay that this feeling is here.

- **Investigate.** Ask yourself, "What really wants my attention right now?" "What am I thinking or believing right now?" Be curious about where this feeling came from so that you can understand it and what message it's bringing you.

- **Nurture.** Offer yourself kindness. You might put a hand to your heart. Say to yourself what you might say to a good friend: "It's okay," "It's not your fault," or even "I'm here for you."

Take a moment to reflect on how you feel:

_____

_____

_____

_____

_____

_____

_____

_____

_____

Now, rate your current level of happiness or ease:

1 2 3 4 5 6 7 8 9 10

Is it different from the level of ease you felt before practicing RAIN? What changed?

_____

_____

_____

_____

_____

_____

_____

_____

_____

_____

_____

RAIN does not get rid of the feeling, but it helps you to process. When you take time to be with the difficult feeling, you will most often feel lighter, calmer, and wiser on the other side. And when you practice this skill, you're not only processing these feelings so you can be more present; you're also modeling healthy emotional regulation for your child.

Helping Your Child with Strong Emotions

How do you normally handle a child's tantrums or difficult feelings?

_____

_____

_____

_____

_____

Children get flooded by strong emotions. It's an inevitable part of childhood, so we need to *expect* children's difficult emotions and *accept* them. When our kids block and repress emotions, those feelings pop out in potentially destructive ways, like exploding at a sibling. Let's agree that we don't want that, any more than we as parents want to block and repress emotions that will later pop out in our interactions with our children. So just as we practice to accept our own emotions, we must seek to accept our children's emotions, and help them to accept their feelings too.

Tantrums, for instance, are children's way of expressing their frustration. It's simply an emotional release. If your child is having a full-on temper tantrum, there's not much you can do to help except stay present, keep them safe, and prevent them from hurting people or damaging objects.

If you are able to stay present, practice becoming grounded in your body, breathing, and accepting your child's big feelings. When you do this, it sends your child some wonderful messages. It tells them, "I see you. I hear you. It's okay for you to have these feelings. I'm here for you. You are safe." When your child feels safe and not abandoned, their big feelings will pass more quickly. Your support also tells them, "I love you no matter what you feel," demonstrating your *unconditional* love. Your silent presence is a powerful response.

When your child's done with their tantrum, practice supporting them with your physical presence. Offer hugs, snuggles, and back rubs. These loving gestures help kids internalize those messages of safety and okay-ness, helping them bounce back sooner.

The following exercise is one to do when your child has a tantrum. Read it carefully so that you have a sense of what to do. You might even write down the basics on an index card to keep with you and help you remember: "Stay with. Notice feelings. We're both safe. Offer hugs."

☐ **Stay with.**

☐ **Notice feelings.**

☐ **We're both safe.**

☐ **Offer hugs.**

PRACTICE: Staying with a Tantrum

When your child's having a tantrum, don't send them to their room or isolate them. Instead, stay with them. Sit or get down low to be at your child's level. Get as close as you feel comfortable, keeping them safe and keeping objects and others safe from them.

Notice your own sensations and thoughts. Are you starting to get tense? If so, take deep, slow breaths with long exhales to calm down your stress response. Notice if you have feelings of wanting to escape. If you can, stay, and be curious about these feelings. Acknowledge them, and focus your attention on slow, calm breathing. You may notice feeling embarrassment (especially if you're in public) or anger. Acknowledge those feelings, then refocus on staying with your child and breathe deeply and slowly. Practice to relax your body.

Say to yourself, "I am helping my child," reminding your nervous system that your child is not a threat. Remember that you are telling your child, "I see you. I hear you. It's okay for you to have these feelings. I'm here for you no matter what. You are safe." Don't pressure yourself to have the right words; remember that staying present is enough. Remember that as you practice staying nonreactive in this challenging moment, you are building your ability to do so again in the future.

As the tantrum subsides, offer hugs and closeness. Don't rush to the next thing. Move slowly and allow time for recovery.

And when you sit mindfully with a tantrum, congratulate yourself! It's *hard*, and it's a big parenting win. Simply riding out this intense emotional expression is a big step in healing for both of you.

The next time you're able to stay with your child through their difficult feelings, take a moment to reflect on how you feel:

Did your child have a different response than with moments of upset in the past? What changed?

_____

_____

_____

_____

_____

_____

_____

_____

_____

_____

_____

Big emotions like anger, fear, and sadness are an inevitable part of life for all of us. Both parents and kids will have intense feelings from time to time; we should expect that as a normal part of life. And when we can mindfully take care of our own big feelings, we will be able to be a grounding presence for our children in their own times of need.

PART 5

Parenting Mindfully

I developed Mindful Parenting out of the tools that I desperately needed when I was failing as a young mom. I turned back to mindfulness to calm my reactivity and found it was incomplete without some training in more skillful communication. I found that I could calm down and have something come out of my mouth (from my parents or culture at large) that *did not* help, like orders and threats. Yet there *is* a language that helps, and what we practice grows stronger. The insights and tools that follow can help you water seeds of skillful communication—and that will grow a strong lifelong relationship with your child.

Modeling in Every Moment

What do we want for our kids? I want my girls to be happy, to feel secure in themselves and confident. I want them to have good relationships with others. More than anything else, I want them to feel comfortable in their own skin—to accept themselves.

What do you want for your kids? Take a moment to think about your answer and write down some ideas.

_____

_____

_____

_____

_____

_____

_____

_____

_____

_____

_____

_____

_____

_____

_____

_____

_____

_____

_____

_____

After you answer that, the big question becomes, "Are you practicing these things in your own life?" You've probably realized already that children tend to be terrible at doing what we *say*, but great at doing what we *do*. And from their infancy, we're teaching our children how to treat others—and how to treat themselves—by the way we treat them. How we respond to our children on a moment-to-moment basis creates a pattern that our children may follow for a lifetime. So, the onus is on us to behave the way we want our children to behave.

What kind of family life would you like to have? How do you want to *feel*? Perhaps you want to feel calm. Or you may want to feel less triggered, and more confident in your choices. And you probably want more cooperation.

Write down your feelings about your family life.

Now, write about how you would like to feel about your family life. What would you like to change? (Or is some of it already changing, if you've practiced other skills you've learned working with this journal?)

_____

_____

_____

_____

_____

_____

_____

_____

_____

_____

_____

_____

_____

It's important to have a clear understanding of what you would like to change. Now, think about how you might make those changes. What are some steps you might take?

How to Connect and Communicate

Our changes on the inside won't make an impact if we're perpetuating old habits and harmful patterns on the outside—with our communication. In Mindful Parenting, I think of this order of operations:

Calm ⇨ **Connect** ⇨ **Communicate** ⇨ **Coach**

It can look like this: When my daughter was two years old, she started having intense tantrums, often several times a day. My husband and I saw her as ticking time bomb, one that could explode at any moment. The anxiety and stress were getting to me. How to cope? I had to learn to ground myself and to listen—this is the Calm step.

What can we do to calm down during a difficult moment? The reason deep breathing is cliché is because it works, so I'm going to share a method here. This breath moves the body out of the "fight, flight, or freeze" response and into the parasympathetic, "rest and relax," response. I use it most mornings to start the day. You can use it to calm down. You can use it to go to sleep. You can use it anytime you notice tension in your body. You can even write the name of this technique down on a sticky note and place strategic reminders about it all around your house.

PRACTICE: 4-7-8 Breathing

Since the "fight, flight, or freeze" response impairs our parenting, we need to engage the opposite "rest and relax" response (through our parasympathetic nervous system) to have access to the whole brain. 4-7-8 Breathing is a technique for deep relaxation conceived by Harvard-trained medical doctor and founder of the Arizona Center for Integrative Medicine Dr. Andrew Weil.[****] Note that while "4-7-8" is one effective breath pattern you can use when you practice, ultimately, the pace doesn't matter. The important part is keeping the exhale longer than the inhale.

Here's how you do it:

1. **Breathe in through your nose for a count of four.**

2. **Hold your breath for a count of seven.** (Note: You can skip the hold if you find it makes you anxious.)

3. **Exhale through your mouth for a count of eight.** Feel free to make an audible "whoosh" sound.

4. **Repeat this pattern of breathing at least four times.**

[****] Weil, A. 2011. *Spontaneous Happiness: A New Path to Emotional Well-Being*. New York: Little, Brown Spark.

Try a round of 4-7-8 breathing.

Now, rate your current stress level:

1 2 3 4 5 6 7 8 9 10

Is this stress level different from your level before you began your practice? What changed?

_____

_____

_____

_____

_____

_____

_____

_____

_____

_____

_____

Do you have other go-to calming tools? What are they?

The Power of Connection

After calming and taking care of ourselves, we need to connect. Relationships with our children are, in some ways, just like other relationships: you need to give them time and attention for them to be strong and connected. Love is not a noun, but a verb. It's something we *do*: a practice, an active choice that we make again and again with the people that are closest to us.

I invite you to set aside one-on-one time with your child to connect, so you can strengthen your bond of love and connection. When your connection is strong, you're more attuned and you reinforce that sense of *caring* about the other. Then parenting becomes easier: each of you is more likely to talk openly, listen with interest, and respect each other's needs. Your child will listen to you more easily. Consciously connecting creates a loving feedback loop.

Right now, how often do you have one-on-one time with your child (or children)?

Are there barriers to you and your kid spending more time together—work, obligations, busy schedules, and more? How do you think you could overcome these barriers, or work around them?

Rate your current level of closeness with your child.

1 2 3 4 5 6 7 8 9 10

And consider: Would you like this to change? Brainstorm a list of ideas to connect with your child.

89

After brainstorming, rank your ideas in order of most appealing:

1. _____

2. _____

3. _____

4. _____

5. _____

6. _____

7. _____

8. _____

9. _____

10. _____

_____

Now, put one of these ideas on your calendar!

Listen to Connect

Relationships are strengthened by being present for the other person—the currency is attention. Every time your child talks to you, they want to make a connection. Those moments are opportunities to strengthen your relationship through simply listening. When you do this, your child can feel truly seen and heard, bolstering your connection.

Yet often we parents listen with half an ear. Kids can have a LOT to say, and we have a lot to do. Life can feel so busy that we don't have time to really listen (and sometimes we truly don't). But sometimes, we don't listen out of a habit of stress. If you can pause in that moment—close the laptop lid, put down the phone, or turn off the oven burner, and look at your child with fresh eyes—you'll nourish the bond that ultimately makes cooperation and family life easier.

When your child wants your attention, how do you usually respond? How do you feel at these times? You might observe yourself for a few days, just as you typically are, as you consider these questions.

Day 1

Day 2

Day 3

We don't have to drop everything and listen 100 percent of the time. Instead, we can aim to practice the middle path of awareness: considering our child's needs *and* our own needs. From there, we can work to meet both.

Put yourself in your child's shoes for a moment. What is their ideal scenario for *you* listening to *them*? What are you doing or not doing? What is your body language? How do you respond to what they say?

After a few days of observation, consider: Are there ways you would like to adjust your responses?

Listen to Be Helpful

When our children come to us with problems (the skinned knee, the argument with a sibling, and so on), often our first, unconscious impulse is to "make the problem go away." We try to do that by dismissing it ("You're fine") or telling our children what to do to solve the problem. These responses are well meant, but unfortunately, they communicate a message of *nonacceptance* of your child's thoughts and feelings. Consider: If you told a friend that you were hurt, and they brushed off your feelings, you'd likely feel dismissed and discouraged. What you intend as problem solving may feel just dismissive and discouraging to your child.

What about offering advice? Many of us have experienced this with adult friends or partners: we need to talk about an issue, and our partner starts telling us what to do—very frustrating! Informing your kids how to solve their problems, which seems so benign, can over time send a message of *no confidence*—that your child *can't* solve problems.

Take a day or two to become aware of how you respond to your child's problems. What kind of communication patterns do you notice?

_____

_____

_____

_____

How does your child respond to your feedback?

_____

_____

_____

_____

_____

_____

_____

_____

_____

_____

_____

If we want to avoid dismissing problems or reflexively offering advice, how do we help instead? Experts in mental and emotional health have been practicing validating feelings for years and it's coming into everyday life with families. Let's explore the practice.

Pay attention mindfully.

• • •

Hear the facts and the underlying feelings.

• • •

Respond with your understanding.

• • •

Express empathy.

When someone has a problem and is upset, reflective listening asks us to guess and put a name to what that person is feeling. When your child is upset, the lower, more emotional part of their brain has taken over. When you name the feeling, it helps bring your child's upper brain—the regions responsible for emotional regulation and decision-making—back into the picture. By responding empathetically to their feelings, whatever those feelings happen to be, you show your child that you really see and hear them.

Imagine your child comes to you with a small injury from the playground. How can you reflectively listen to their feelings?

Now, imagine your child is upset at their sibling or friend. Write out your reflective listening response.

Now, write down some real problems that your child has come to you with.

And now, write out an empathetic, reflective listening response for each one:

Responding with empathy does not mean that you agree with your child, or that you don't hold boundaries with your child. It simply means that you validate their feelings. You see and hear them no matter what. That is the very definition of unconditional love.

Reflect on some of your experiences with reflective listening, once you've had the chance to practice the skill at least a few times. How does it shift the emotional temperature of a situation? Does it feel natural or like a new language that you need to practice? Could you practice reflective listening with anyone else in your life?

What are some common situations in your life that could benefit from reflective listening?

Take Care of Your Needs

Our needs as parents are varied and range from the basics of nourishing food, regular exercise, and a good night's sleep to deeper needs like intimacy, joy, and purpose. These bump up against kids' natural immaturity—while going about meeting their needs, they inevitably impinge on some of our own. That's when we need to hold boundaries, because parents' needs are just as important as children's needs. When we neglect our needs, burnout can come quickly, and then we are not present or effective parents.

This assessment will help you become aware of where you are neglecting your own needs. Go through and evaluate your life now, using the scale below. Note this assessment isn't exhaustive, but it may help you spark ideas.

3 = Rock on! You do this frequently and well.

2 = You do this occasionally, or you're okay at it.

1 = You barely do this.

0 = You never do this, or it hasn't even occurred to you.

PHYSICAL SELF-CARE

I eat regular, healthy meals. **0 1 2 3**

I enjoy regular exercise that feels good to my body. **0 1 2 3**

I get enough sleep. **0 1 2 3**

I get outside every day. **0 1 2 3**

MENTAL/EMOTIONAL SELF-CARE

I spend time with friends. **0 1 2 3**

I make time for self-reflection and stress-reduction. **0 1 2 3**

I have healthy ways to comfort and soothe myself. **0 1 2 3**

I express my frustration in healthy ways. **0 1 2 3**

I do things that bring me enjoyment. **0 1 2 3**

RELATIONSHIP SELF-CARE

I spend time with my partner away from my kids regularly. **0 1 2 3**

I ask for help when I need it. **0 1 2 3**

I call or see my relatives and/or faraway friends. **0 1 2 3**

I prioritize time alone when I need it. **0 1 2 3**

OVERALL SELF-CARE

I practice gratitude. **0 1 2 3**

I connect with what is meaningful to me. **0 1 2 3**

I pay attention to everyday beauty in the world around me. **0 1 2 3**

I take time to pause when I need it. **0 1 2 3**

This assessment may bring up a variety of emotions for you. You may be shocked at how you've been treating yourself. Don't feel pressured to act right now. Instead, take some time to journal and reflect.

What are your best areas of self-care?

_____

_____

_____

_____

_____

Which areas do you want to improve?

_____

_____

_____

_____

_____

Now, pick the area you most want to improve on, and start there.

Prioritizing our own needs can be difficult, particularly in a culture shaped by (patriarchal) ideas that celebrate the "self-sacrificing" parent. With some mindful awareness, we can see the reality that our burnout doesn't help anyone. What our children need most is a grounded, loving parent and a model of how to live with steadiness and ease. That won't happen if we don't prioritize meeting our own needs. As they say on airplanes, we must put our own oxygen masks on first before we help others.

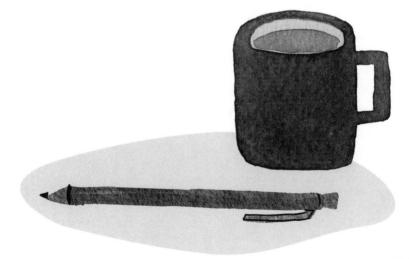

Express Yourself Honestly and Effectively

So, what do we do when our kids impinge upon our needs? When our toddler says, "No!" to school, but we have to be at work? When we just need some quiet and rest and our preschooler wants to play with the karaoke toy? Stepping back into the big picture, we can see that our cultural mindset is often *I have to make you do what I want you to do*. Although it may be unconscious, we often have the intention of *manipulating* our children, rather than coaching them. Thus, the most common (unskillful) language we hear ourselves use with our kids is orders and threats.

A toddler's or preschooler's day can be filled with commands: *Get in the car now. Put your shoes on. Take your shoes off. Put that down.* Children, like humans of every age, don't like to have their every move directed, so they resist. When kids resist, we often resort to threats: *If you don't get in the car right now, we won't stop for ice cream. If you don't put away the toy, I'm going to throw it away.* This may "work" in the moment, but threats make kids feel coerced and manipulated. It ultimately backfires because it makes kids *less* likely to voluntarily cooperate in the future.

Take a few days to listen to your language and the language of others around children. What do you observe?

_____

_____

_____

Imagine that you are a small child, and an adult is ordering you around, then threatening to take away something you love. How does it feel to be on the receiving end of this kind of language?

Sometimes all it takes to shift to more skillful language is a change in perspective. We can shift how we coach our kids on everything from table manners to getting out the door by asking ourselves, *How would I say it to my friend's child?*

Write down three everyday moments where you must hold boundaries with your child:

1. _____

2. _____

3. _____

Now, write down what you would say in those moments if you were talking to your friend's child.

1. _____

_____

_____

_____

_____

_____

_____

2.

3.

We don't need to be harsh when we set limits. We can be *firm and kind*.

Not only that, but we can also add a bit of *fun* into the mix. In *Raising Good Humans*, I list several ways to have some fun while holding boundaries, from pretending to be a robot (or alien, or cowboy), to singing songs, to acting as though you can't do basic things ("Oh no, I forgot how to leave this park and I can't find the exit! Is it here [bumping into tree]?"). Summoning the energy to be playful instead of serious and demanding pays dividends in joy and connection later.

Look back at the three moments you often hold boundaries above. Brainstorm some ways that you could respond playfully in those moments.

Solve Problems Mindfully

Our traditional ways of solving conflicts in the family also cause resistance: the parent "puts their foot down" to enforce a solution through punishment or threat of punishment. In this way, the parent "wins" and the child "loses," which causes resentment to build in the child. It also doesn't teach our children better behavior; in fact, it promotes lying and sneaking around to avoid punishment.

Were you punished as a child? How did it make you feel? What did you learn at the time?

_____

_____

_____

_____

_____

_____

_____

_____

How do you currently resolve conflicts with your child? How does this method of conflict resolution affect you? Your child?

Conflicts are normal and inevitable. When we process a conflict by talking and listening, it can ultimately bring us closer together than if there had been no problems at all. How do we do that? Instead of win-lose problem solving, we can practice *win-win* problem solving.

Here's how it works. Most conflicts arise because of a clash between kids' needs and parents' needs; what if we could instead get *everyone's* needs met? We usually have conflicting *solutions* on how to solve a problem. When my daughter sings loudly while I'm trying to focus on writing an email, my solution is for her to be quiet, but that doesn't meet her needs. Instead, I could acknowledge the conflict and invite her into a dialogue: "I can't focus when you sing loudly here. I need some quiet and it looks like you need to sing. How can we get everyone's needs met?" Maybe she'll decide to go into another room for a while to sing, or head out to the backyard. When we get to the level of underlying needs, there are many different solutions.

Think of a recent conflict that arose with your child.

What were your child's needs?   **What were your needs?**

How could you have acknowledged the feelings in the conflict and invited your child into a dialogue? Write down the script of what you could have said:

_____

_____

_____

_____

_____

_____

_____

_____

_____

_____

_____

_____

_____

_____

_____

_____

_____

_____

_____

_____

_____

_____

_____

_____

_____

_____

(For a deeper dive into win-win problem solving, go to *Raising Good Humans* or the Mindful Parenting Course. It engages kids in the process of problem solving, which empowers children and makes them much more likely to cooperate because they're getting their needs met—and teaches them one of the most valuable life skills there is!)

Supporting Your Peaceful Home

Your schedule and home environment can make parenting easier or add to your parenting stress. Children thrive in an environment that is predictable and easy for them to navigate. Because so much of our children's lives is beyond their control, it helps them enormously to be able to orient themselves within a stable rhythm. If they know what to expect from their days, they are much less likely to resist at each step.

What is your daily home rhythm like? How do you start and end your days? Does your child know what to expect after lunch? How can you help your child remember what to expect?

What is your weekly home rhythm like? Does your child know what to expect? How can you help your child remember what to expect?

One of the most important things we can do for our children is protect their time for free, imaginative play. This is the true "work" of childhood in which kids master emotional regulation and tackle their fears and phobias. A rushed schedule packed full of activities does not allow for this; instead, it promotes stress.

How many hours a day does your child have for unstructured, free play versus structured, adult-managed activities? Are there structured activities you could drop to allow more time for free play? What are other ways you can protect down time in your lives?

Simplify for a Mindful Home

Our homes can make a big impact on our parenting, and one of the biggest challenges to parenting mindfully is the problem of *too much*. We struggle with stress from packed schedules and an overabundance of stuff. Yet we don't often recognize it as a problem until we're overwhelmed.

Contrary to popular culture's "more is better" idea, children are happier and more creative in a simplified environment than a space cluttered with toys. Children thrive in rooms that are simple and tidy, with things they need at their level to facilitate "I do it myself!"

Imagine that you are your child and go around your rooms from their point of view. Are you able to get yourself a glass of water? Can you reach a towel to clean up? Can you hang up your own jacket? What could be more accessible?

Contrary to what commercial culture teaches, children find tons of toys to be overwhelming; there are just too many choices, and it's stressful to clean up. Chances are, you can easily remove half to three-quarters of your child's toys (just to a holding space for now, in case you need to retrieve a particularly beloved toy) and your child will be delighted with the decluttered space.

Look at the toys that are available. Can your child put them away independently in five minutes? If not, then you most likely have too many toys out. Where can you reduce toys in your home?

What else can you simplify in your home? Closets, bedrooms, the kitchen, or in hallways? Imagine your home decluttered and easier to care for. What does that feel like? How does it affect your day-to-day life?

Your Mindful Parenting Journey

Throughout this journal you've reflected on yourself, your child, and your home. You've watered the seeds of awareness, compassion, and skillful communication—which will grow, blossom, and give fruit. This fruit, our loving, positive relationship with our children, can offer us more happiness, meaning, and fulfillment than anything else. You don't have to be perfect on this journey. Instead, I invite you to commit to *beginning anew*, again and again. Commit to returning to these practices, to yourself, to your loving intention to become steady and present.

Let's complete this portion of your mindful parenting journey with one of the most powerful tools there is: *gratitude*. What are you grateful for in your child? What are you grateful for in your family life?

Reflect on where you were at the start of this journal and compare it to where you are now. Do you feel differently? Think differently? What has changed for you?

Inside each of us is a voice of wisdom, a compassionate and grounded voice that can lead us with light and steadiness. Take a moment to be still and breathe with the intention of opening up to that voice. What is your direction forward? How will you practice being present on a daily, weekly, and seasonal basis? What is your most sincere intention for you and your child (or children)?

What else are you taking away from the work you've done in this journal?

I honor you and thank you for taking
the time with this guided journal.

Your reflection and the work you've
done here will positively impact
not just your own family but
also your community and
generations to come.

Hunter Clarke-Fields, MSAE, is creator of Mindful Parenting, host of the *Mindful Parenting* podcast, and author of *Raising Good Humans*. She coaches parents on how to cultivate mindfulness in their daily lives and cooperation in their families. Hunter has more than twenty years of experience in meditation practices, and has taught thousands worldwide.

More Books by Hunter Clarke-Fields

With this essential guide, you'll see how changing your own "autopilot reactions" can create a lasting positive impact—not just for your kids, but for generations to come.

ISBN 978-1684033881 / US $16.95

This "go-to" daily guide offers 50 simple ways to press pause, stop reacting, and start parenting with intention.

ISBN 978-1648481420 / US $18.95

🌼 **new**harbinger**publications**

1-800-748-6273 / newharbinger.com